Light and Shade Series
Book 1

Roditch

Dedicated to Nan

She has both:

Copyright © Roditch 2022

She lives on the Moon
and reflects the Sun

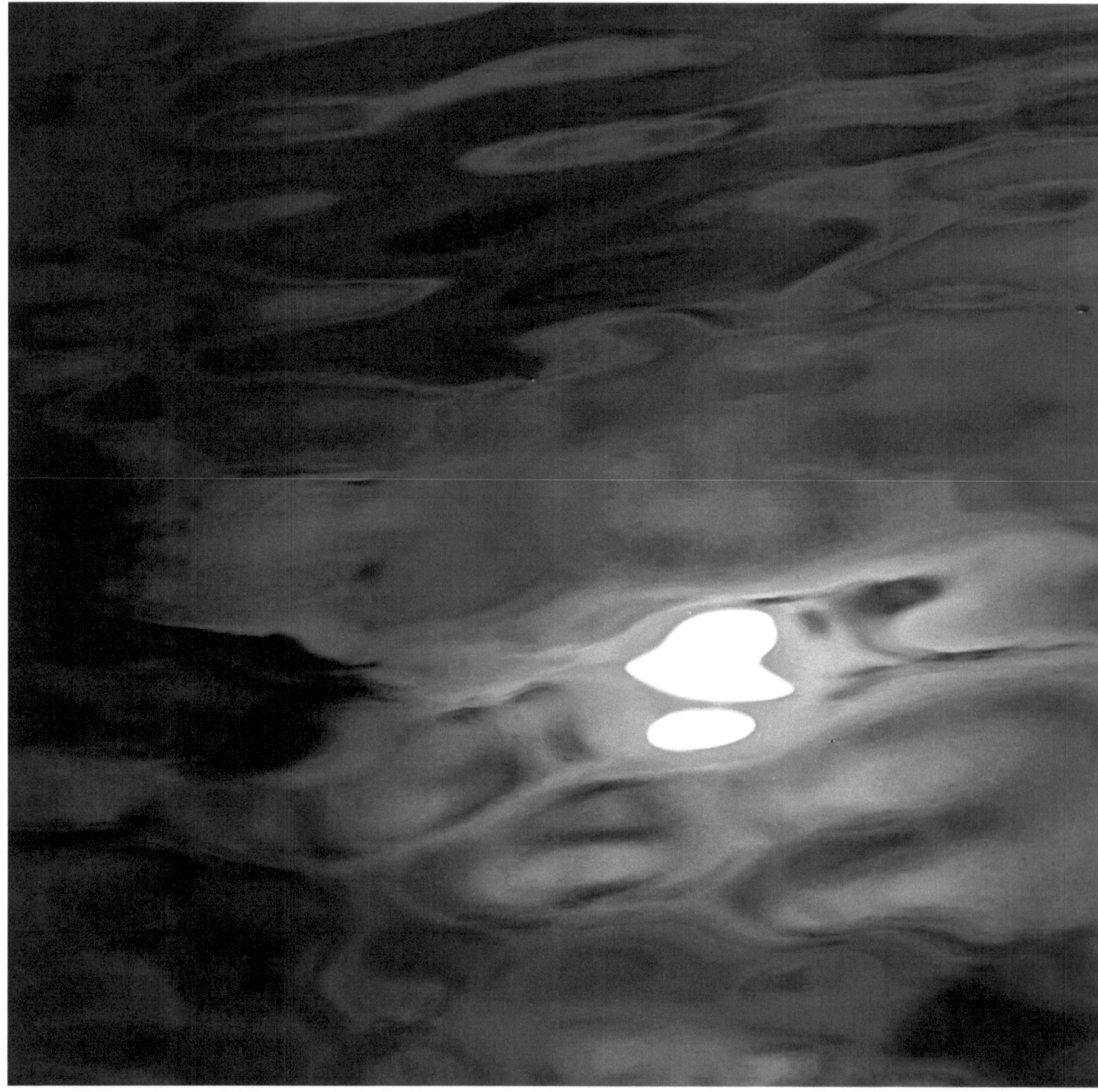

Lighten your heart
and love your neighbour

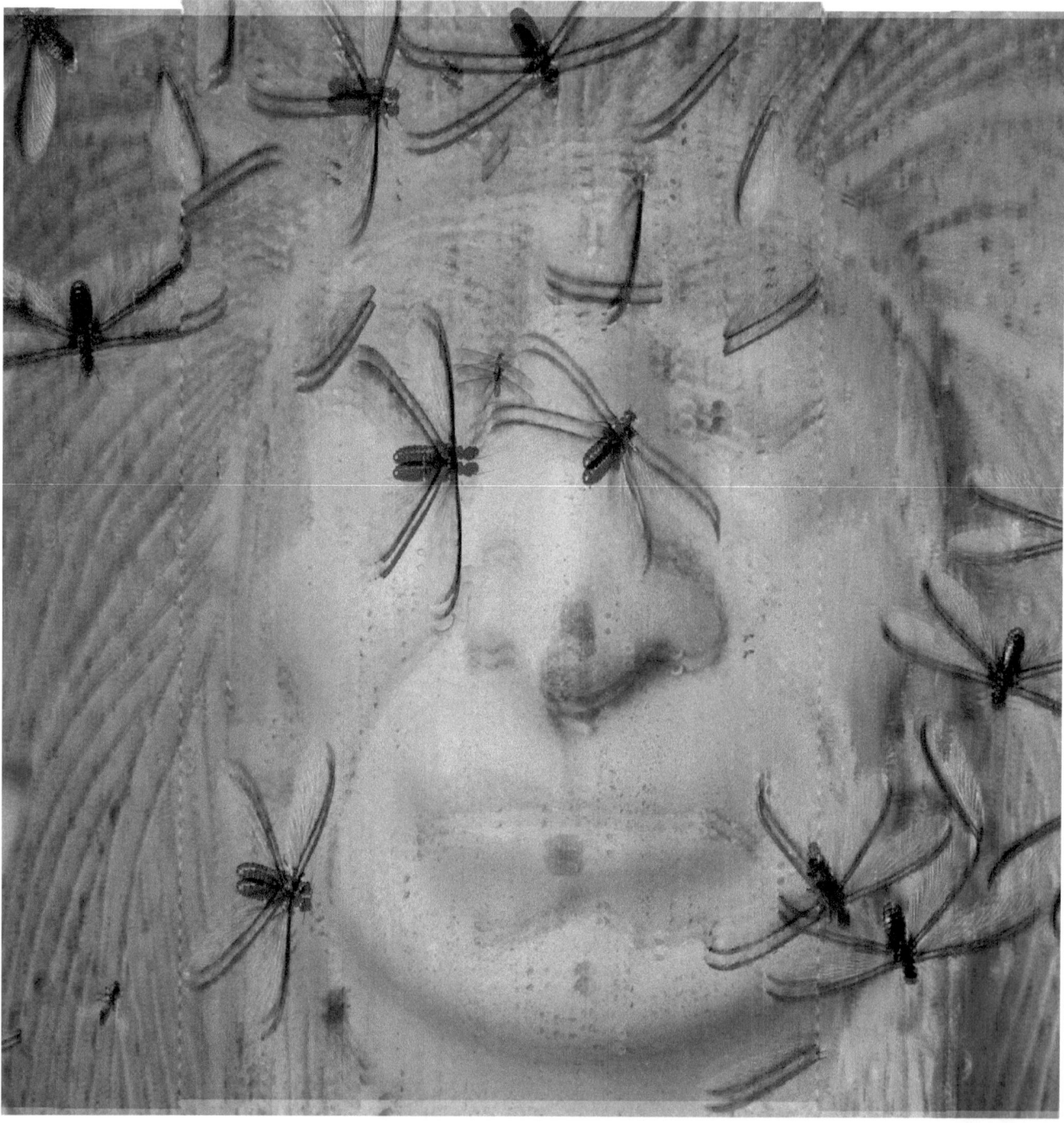

Heaven is a place to go
when you are sad

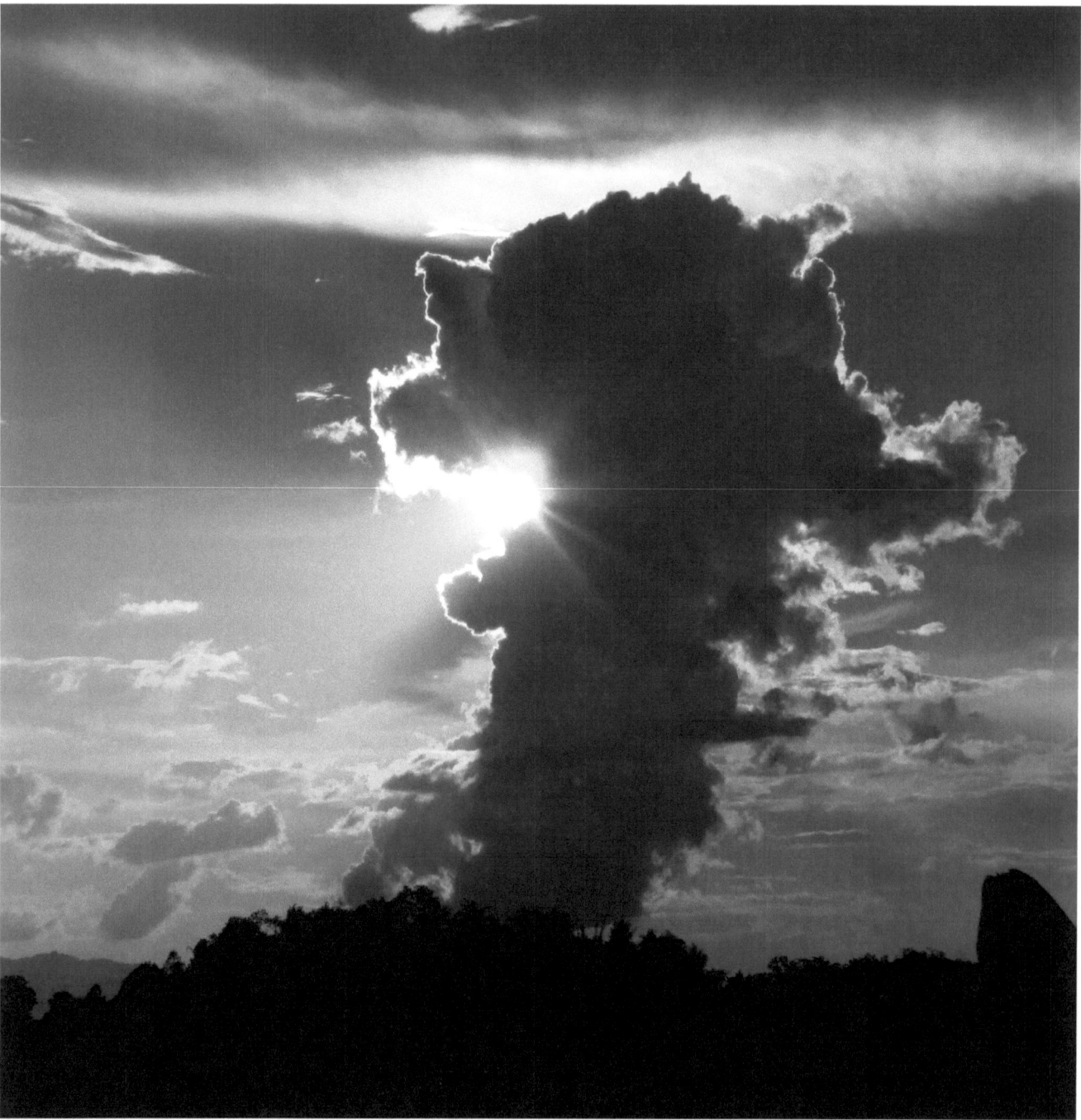

Sleeping with my eyes open

The I ~~before~~ the AI

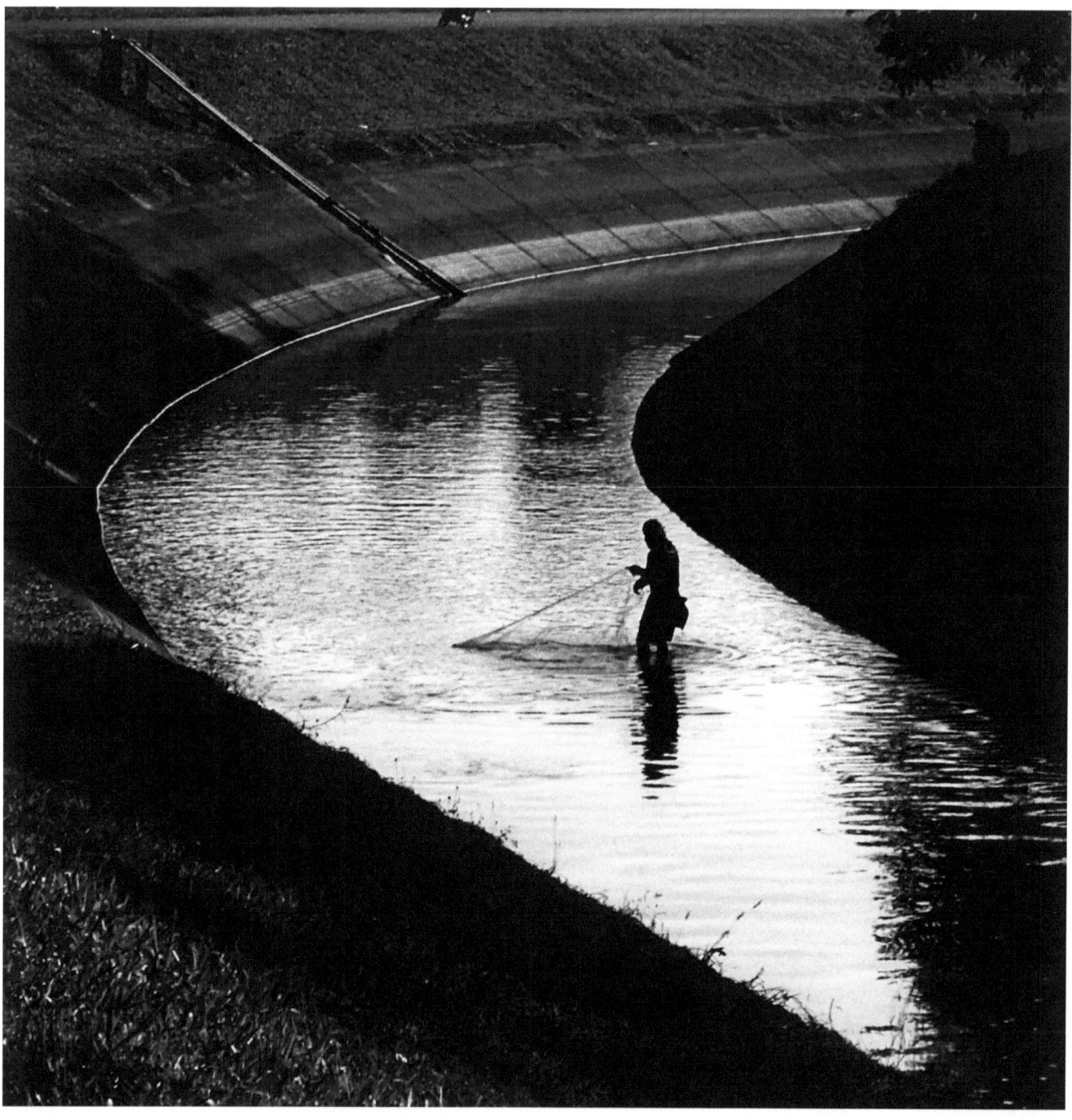

Happiness in my state of being

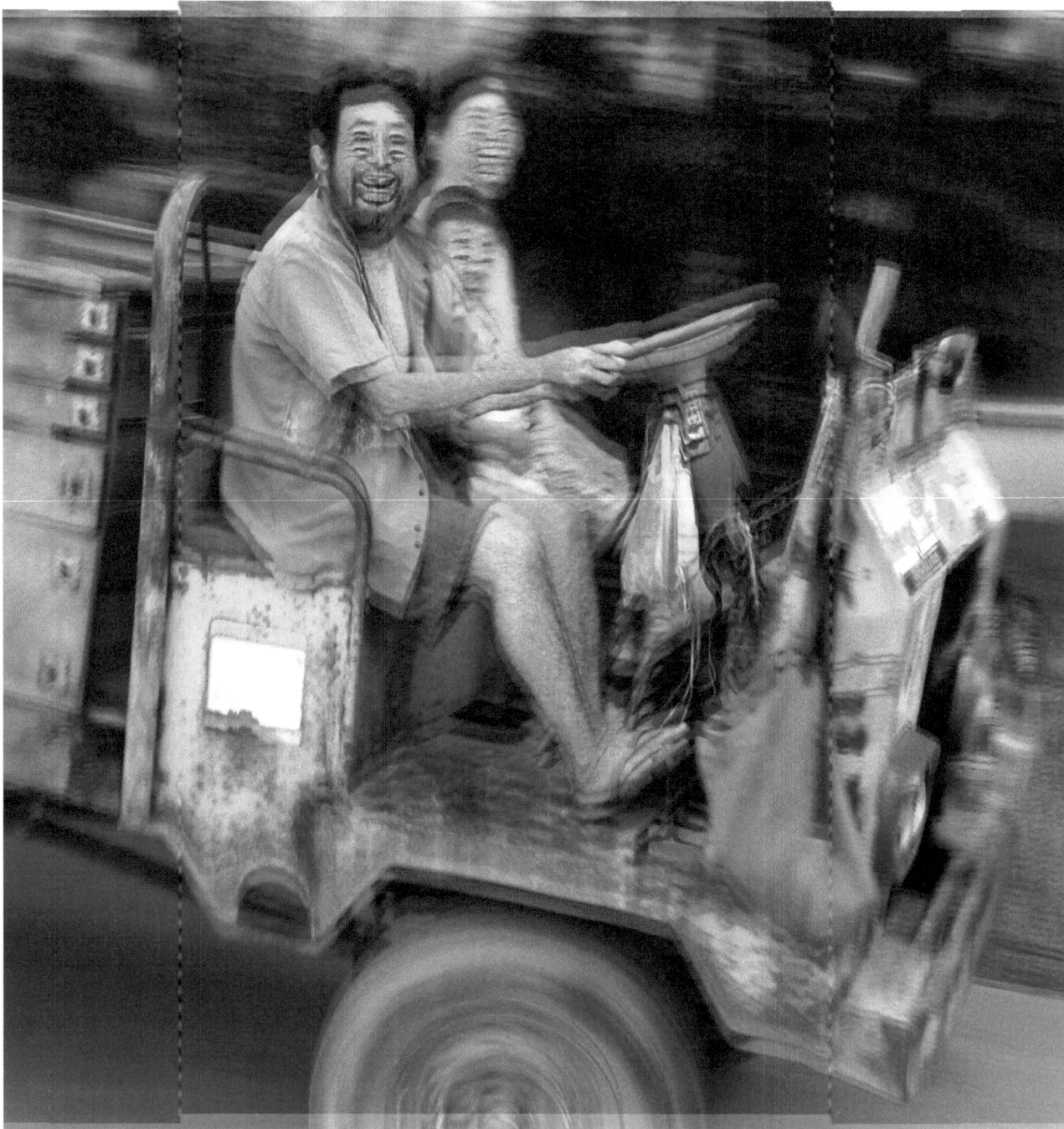

Never alone for long

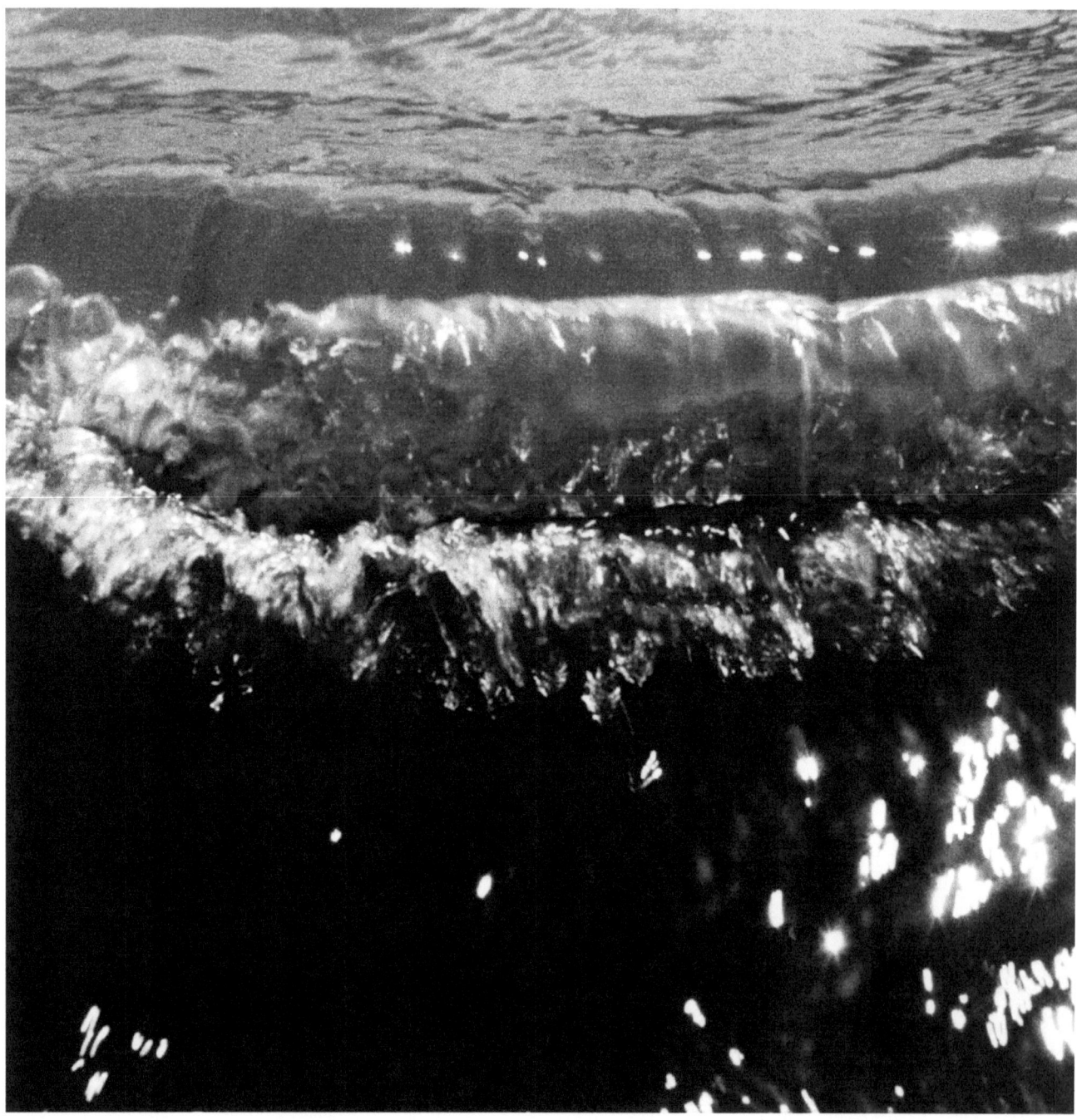

No life without the giver

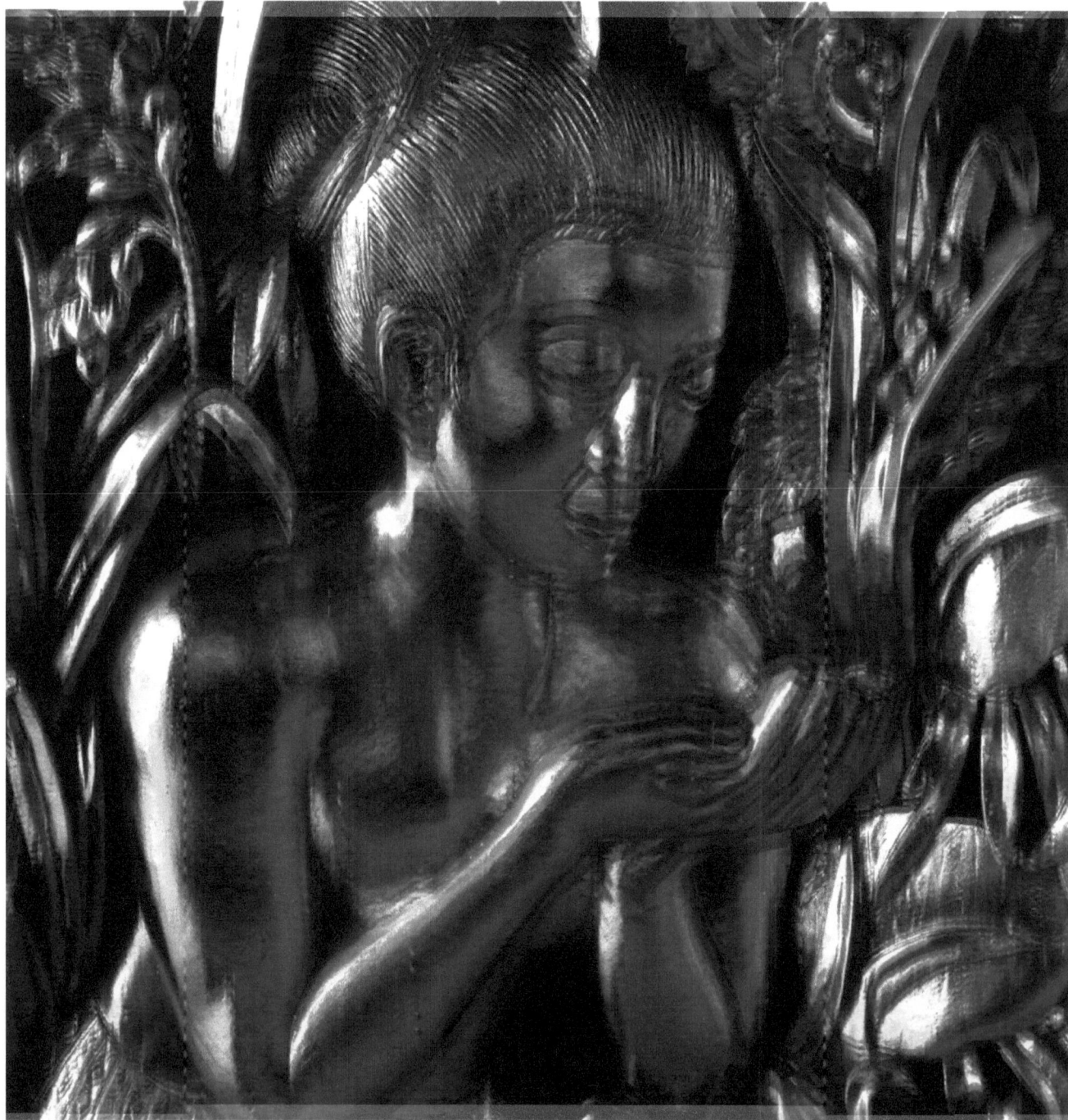

Speaking in tongues

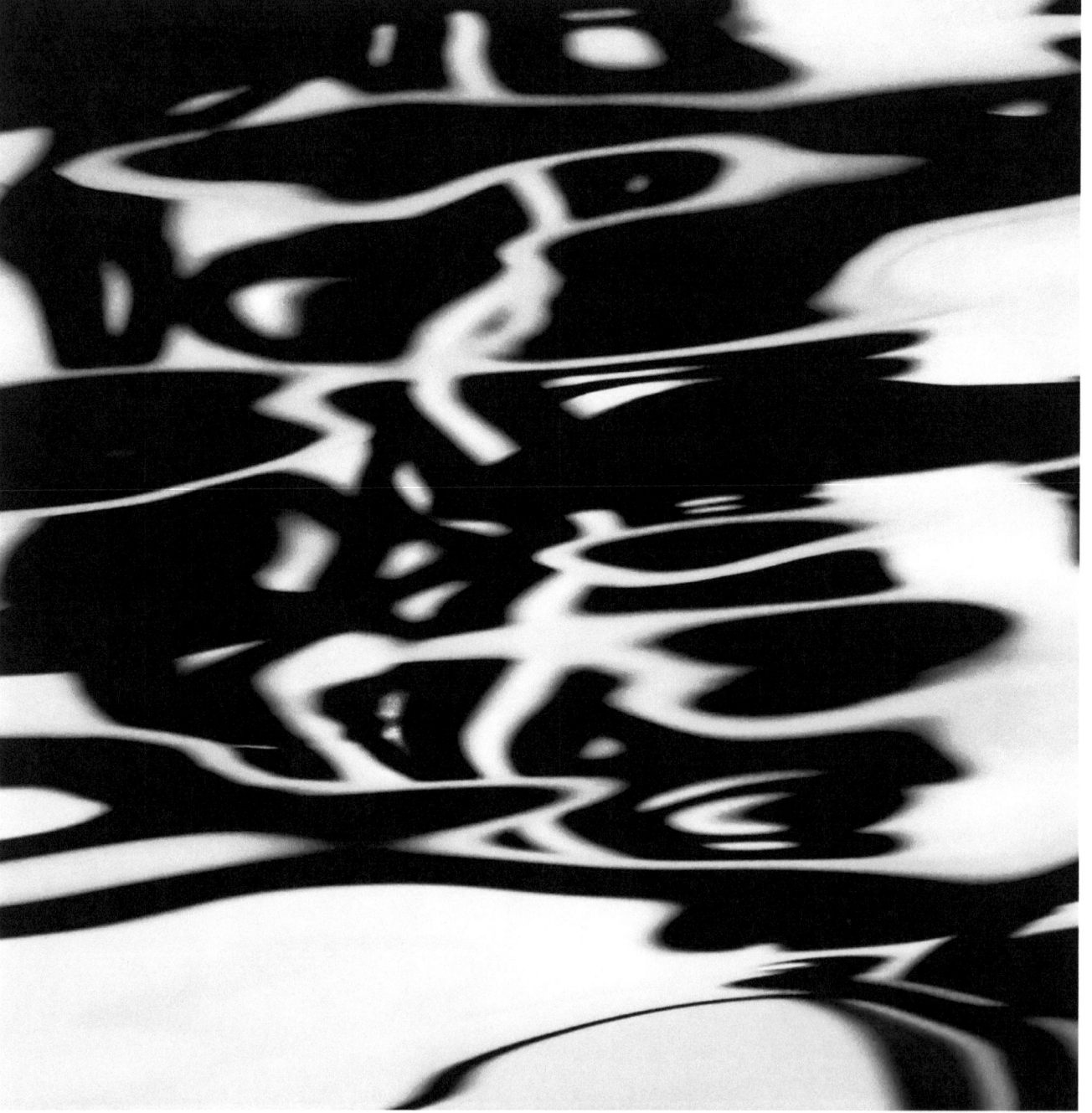

I am a wind in the willows

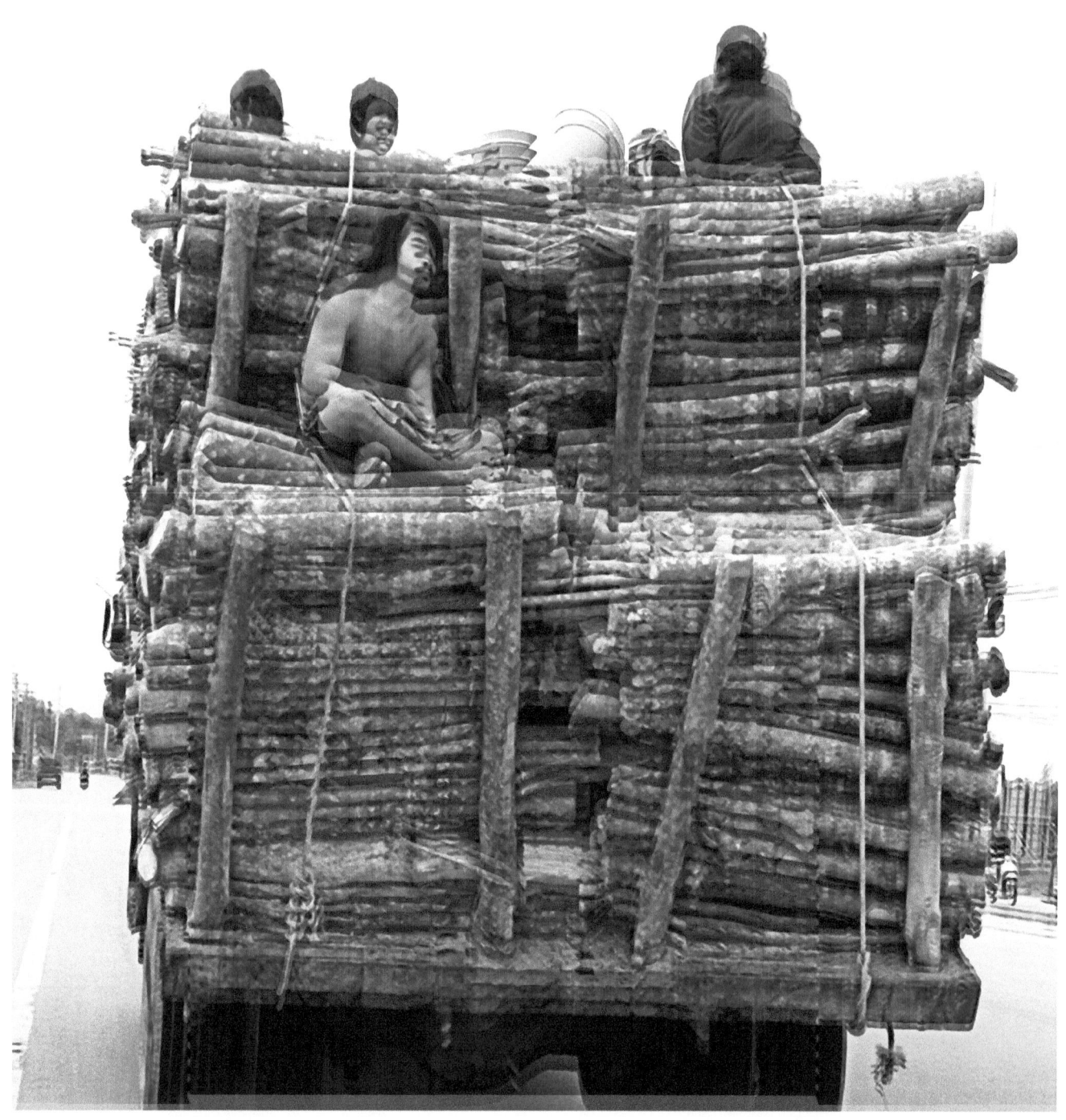

Touch and be loved

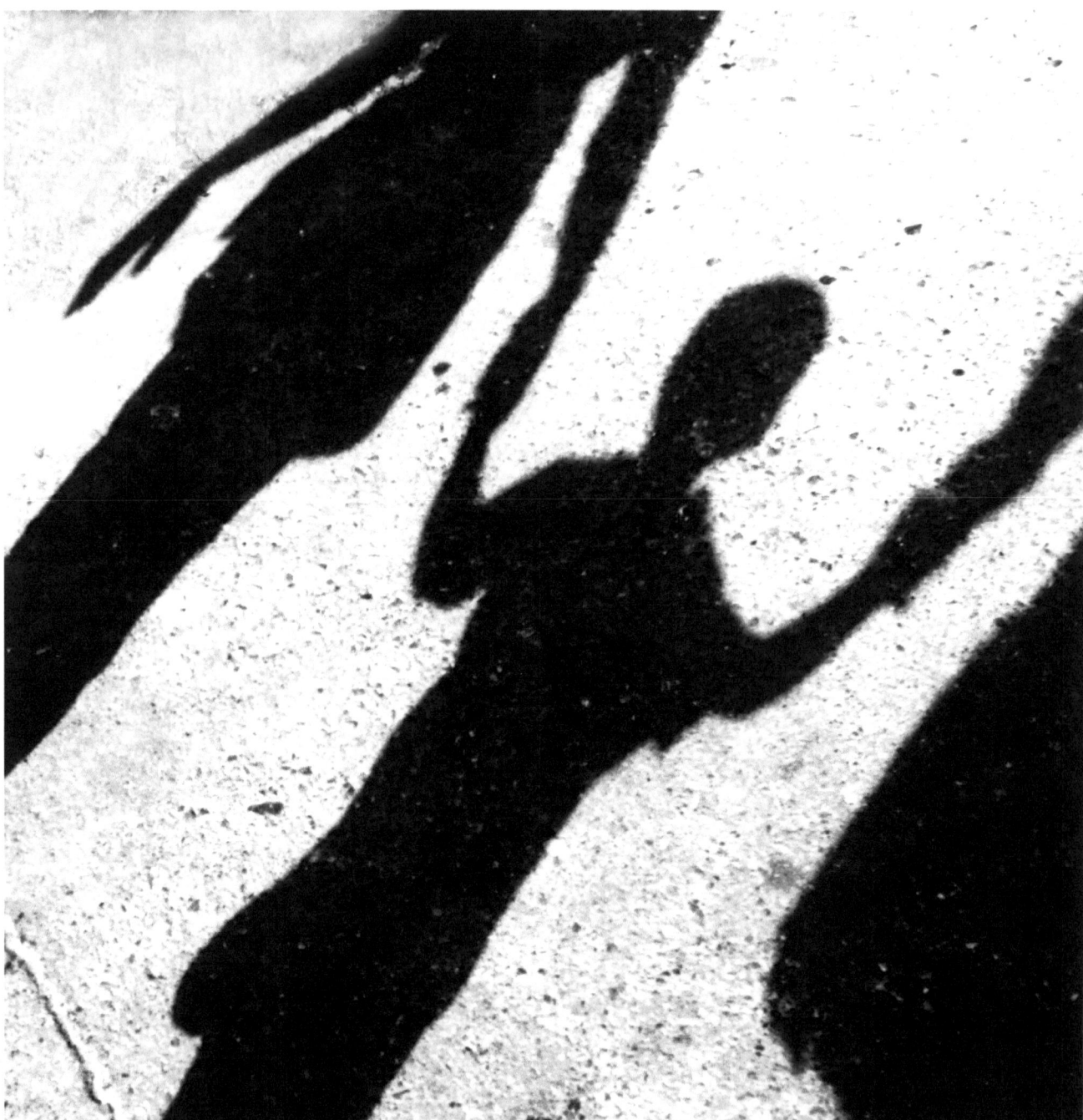

Drifting words

I am here

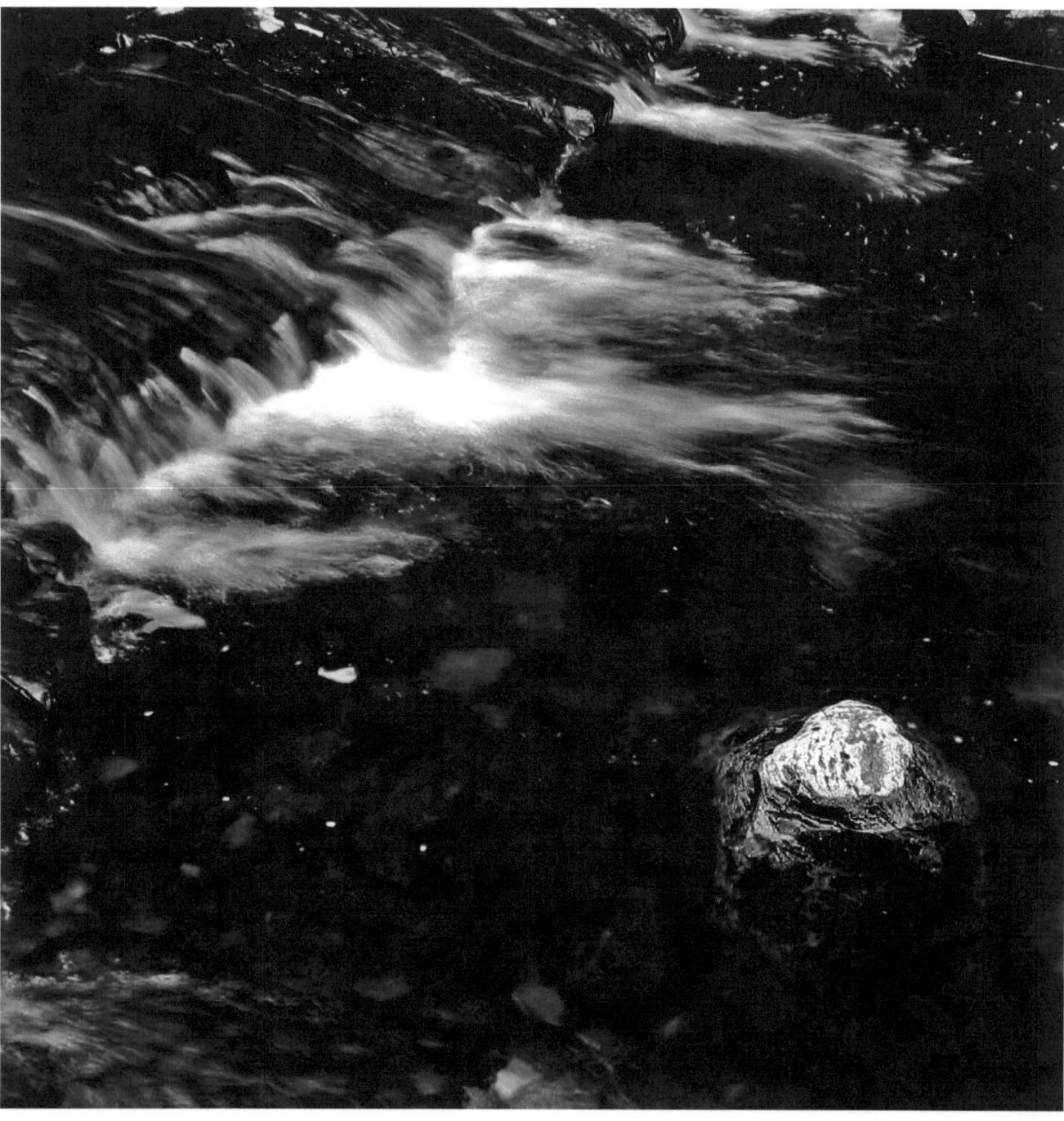

Stop working for the Devil

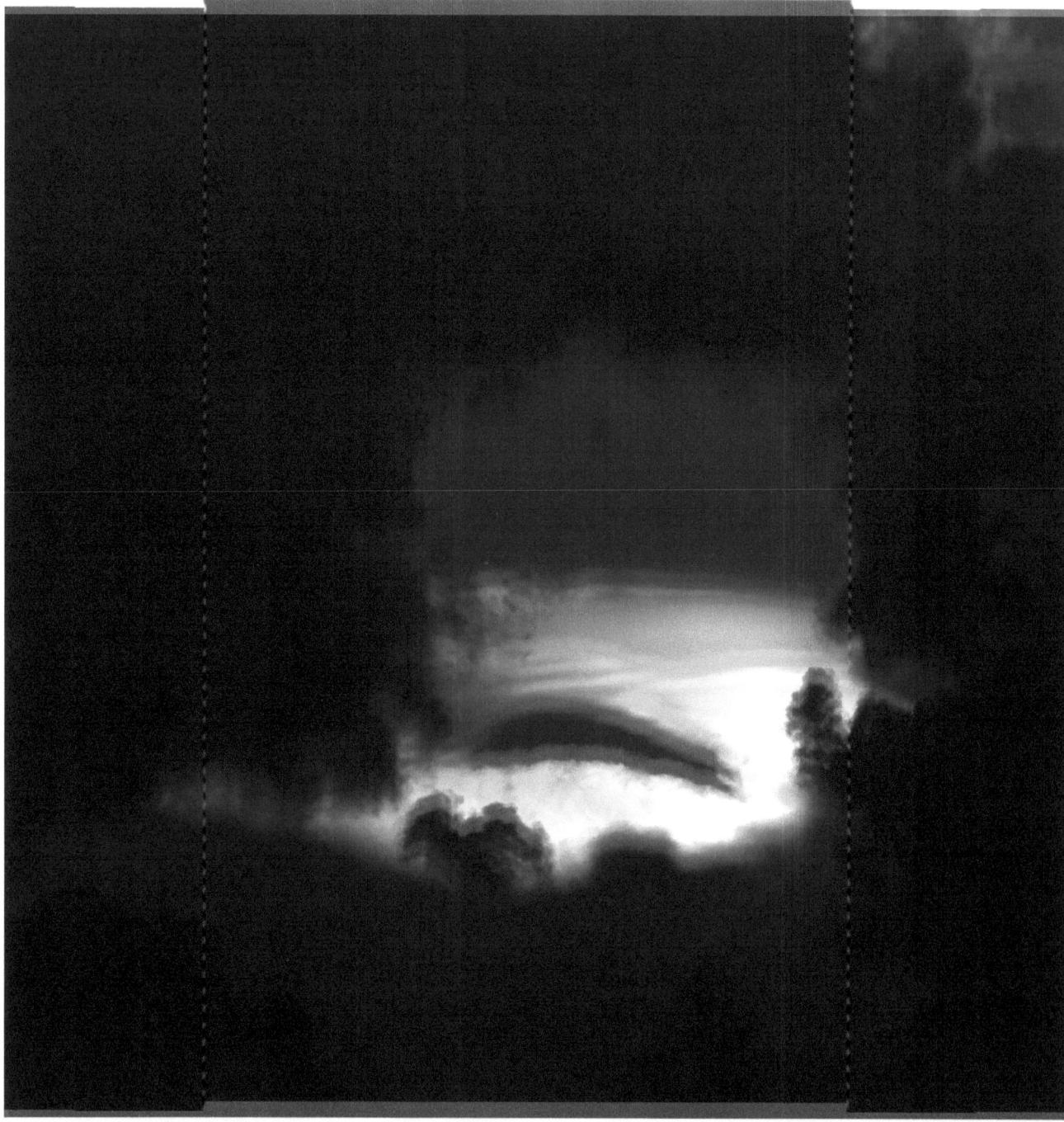

Born to grow

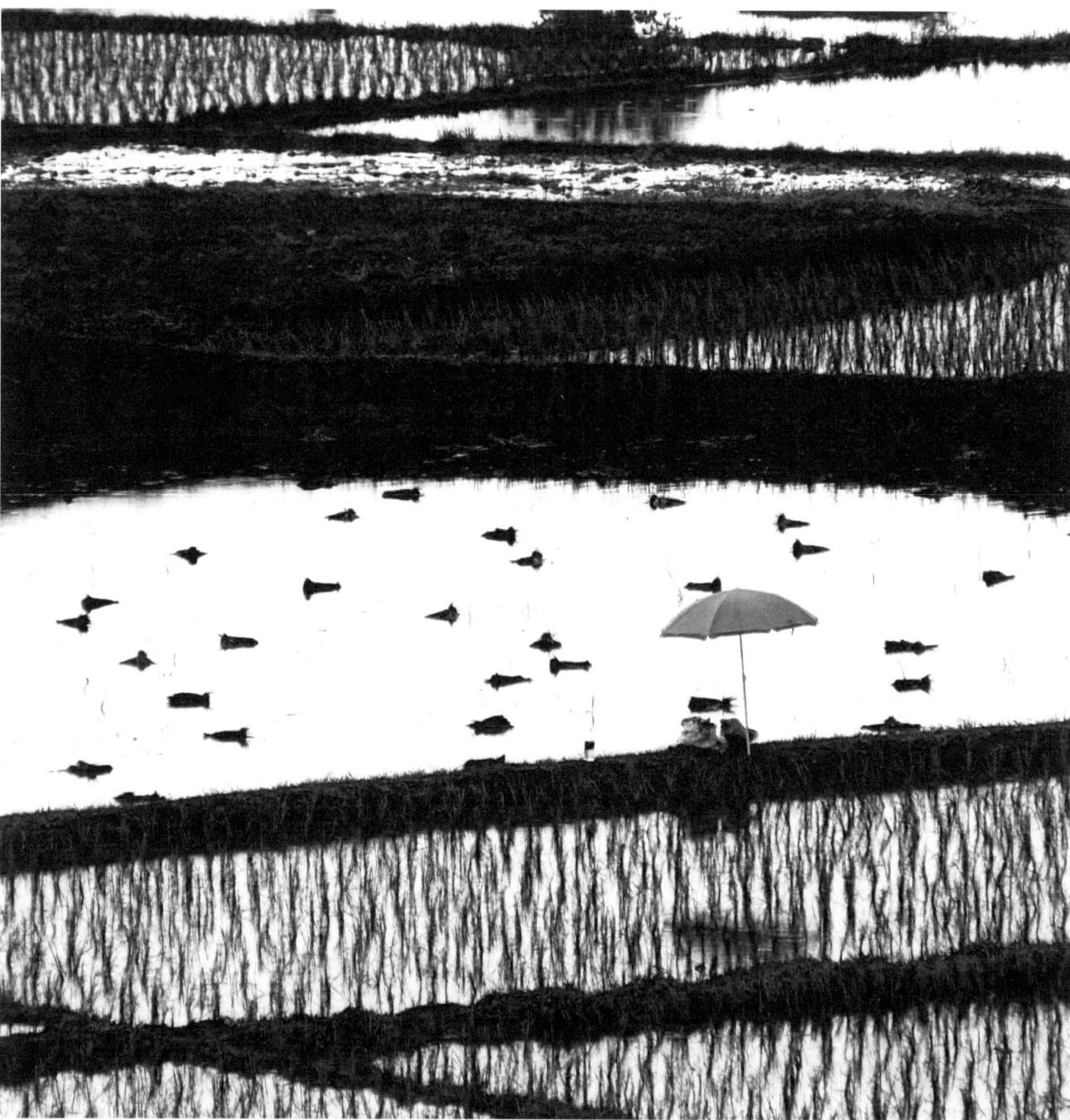

The watcherer

All equal under it

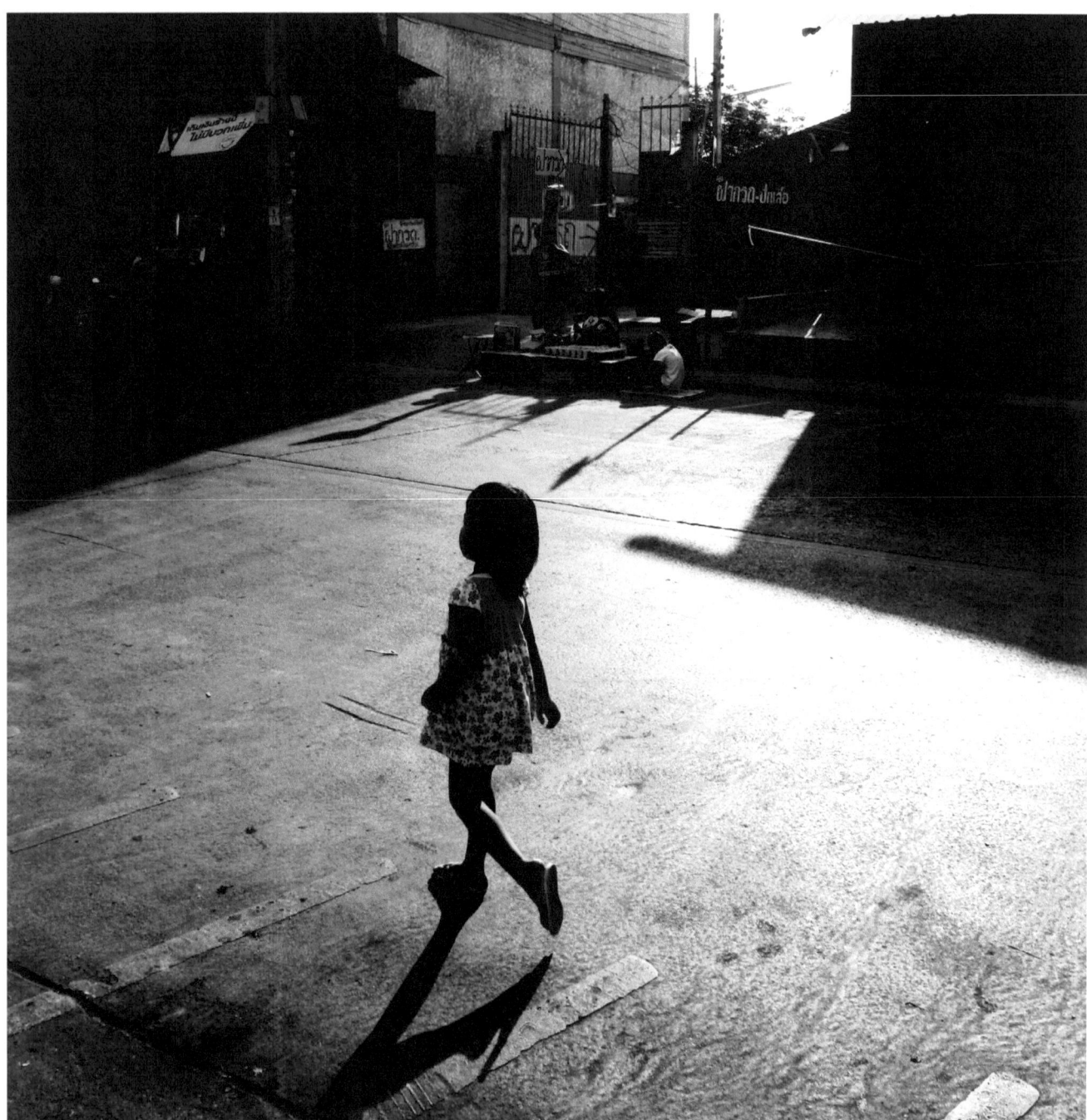

Brass heart

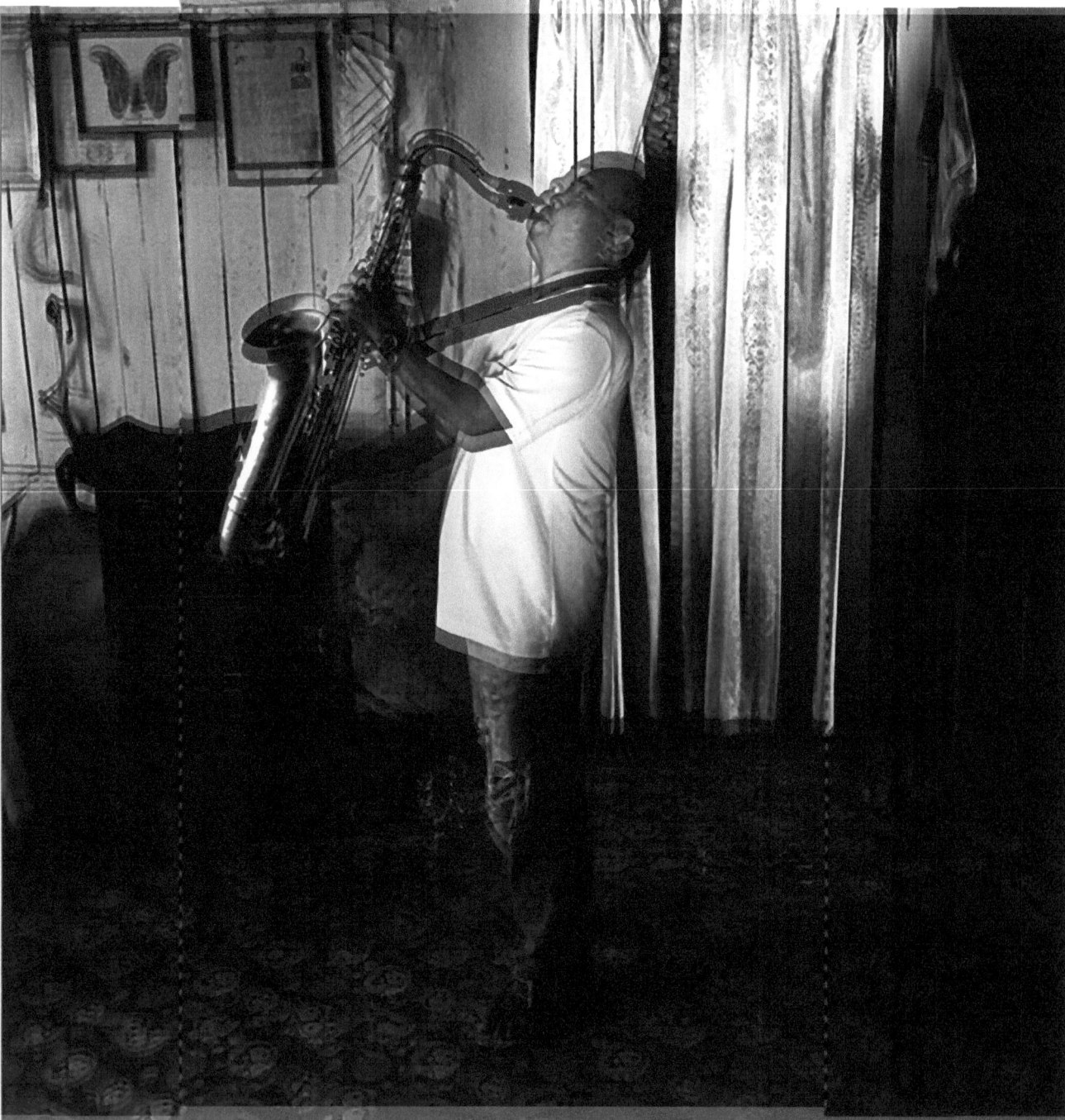

Going home

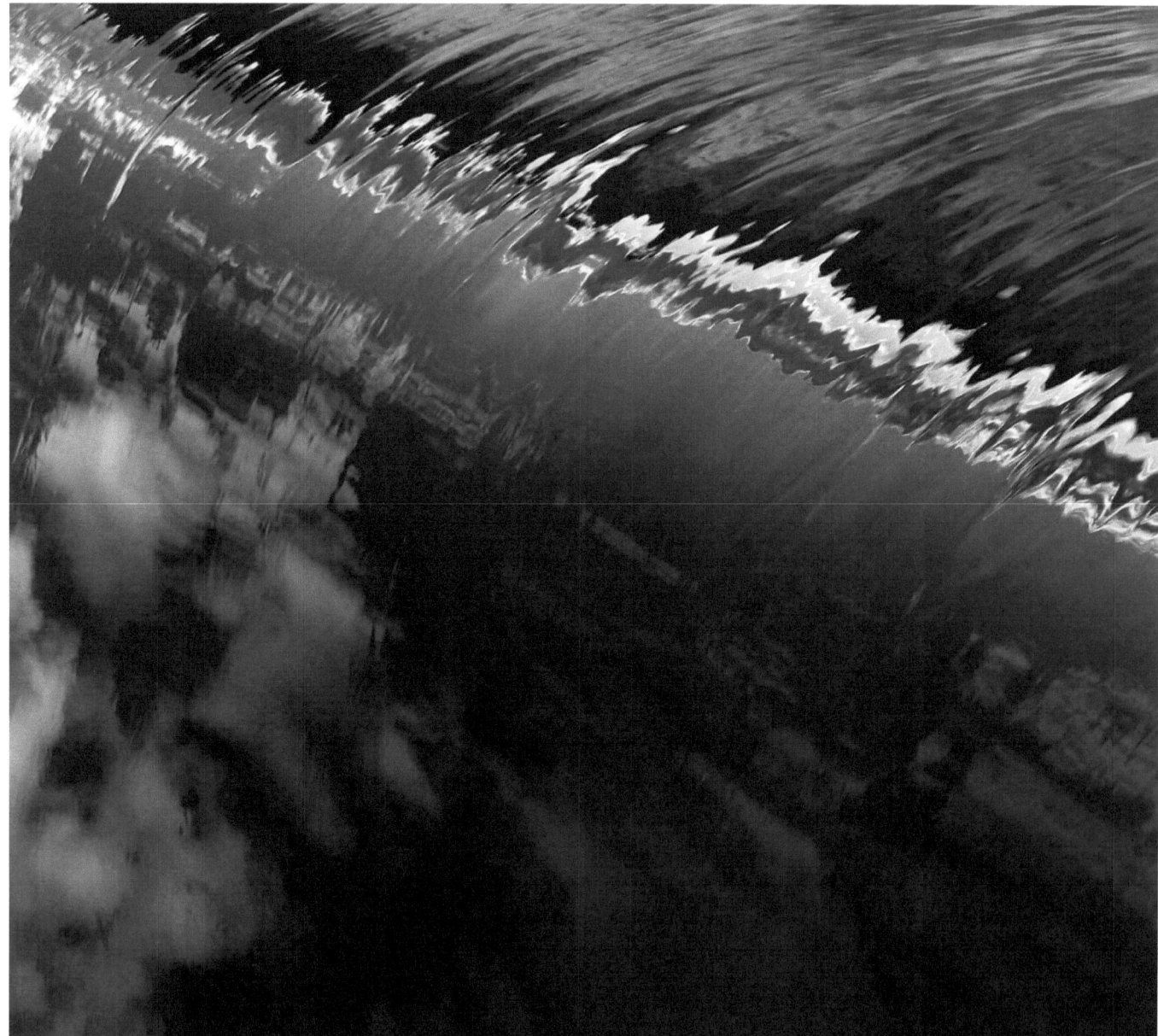

I am with me

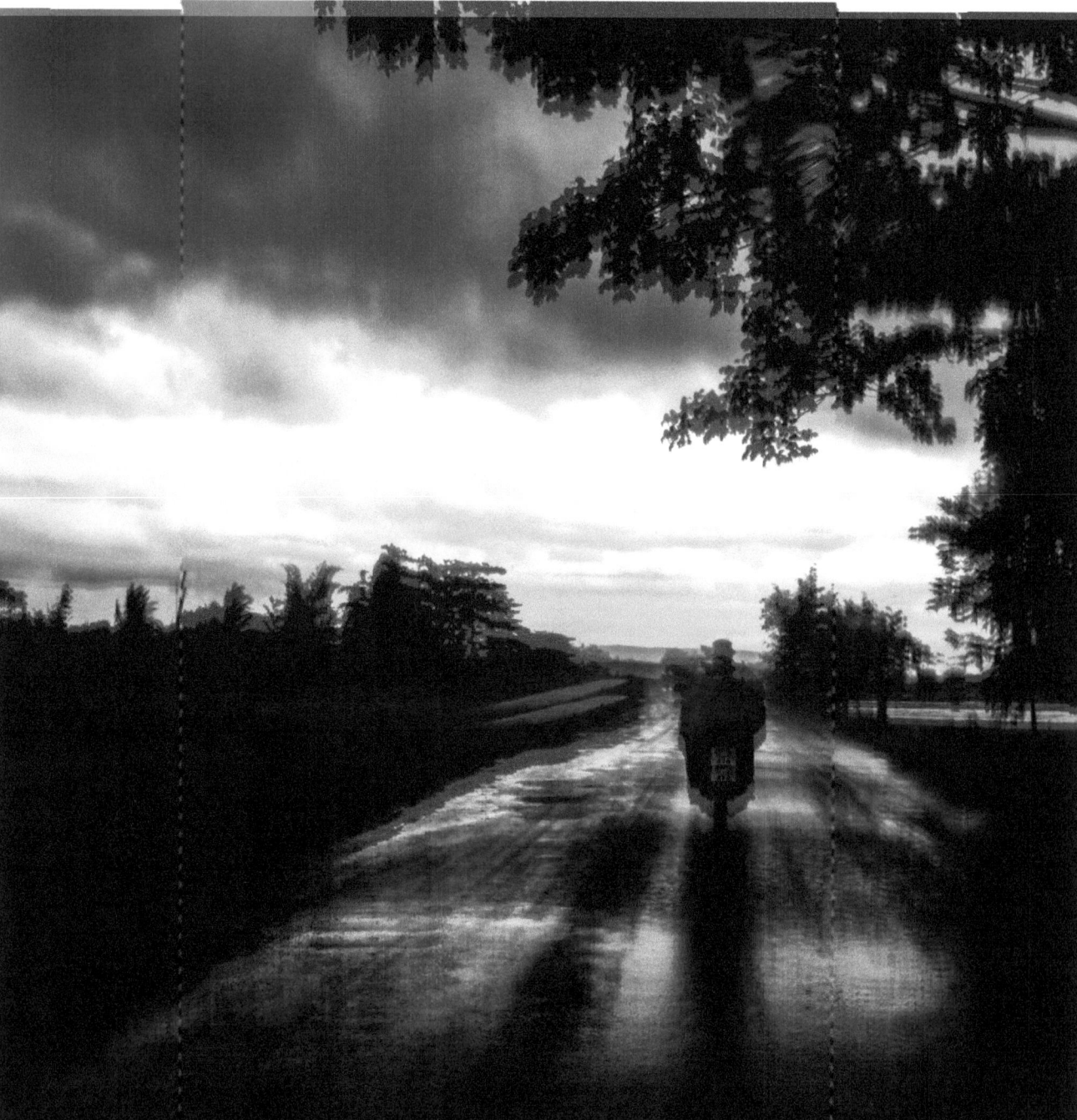

Light, action

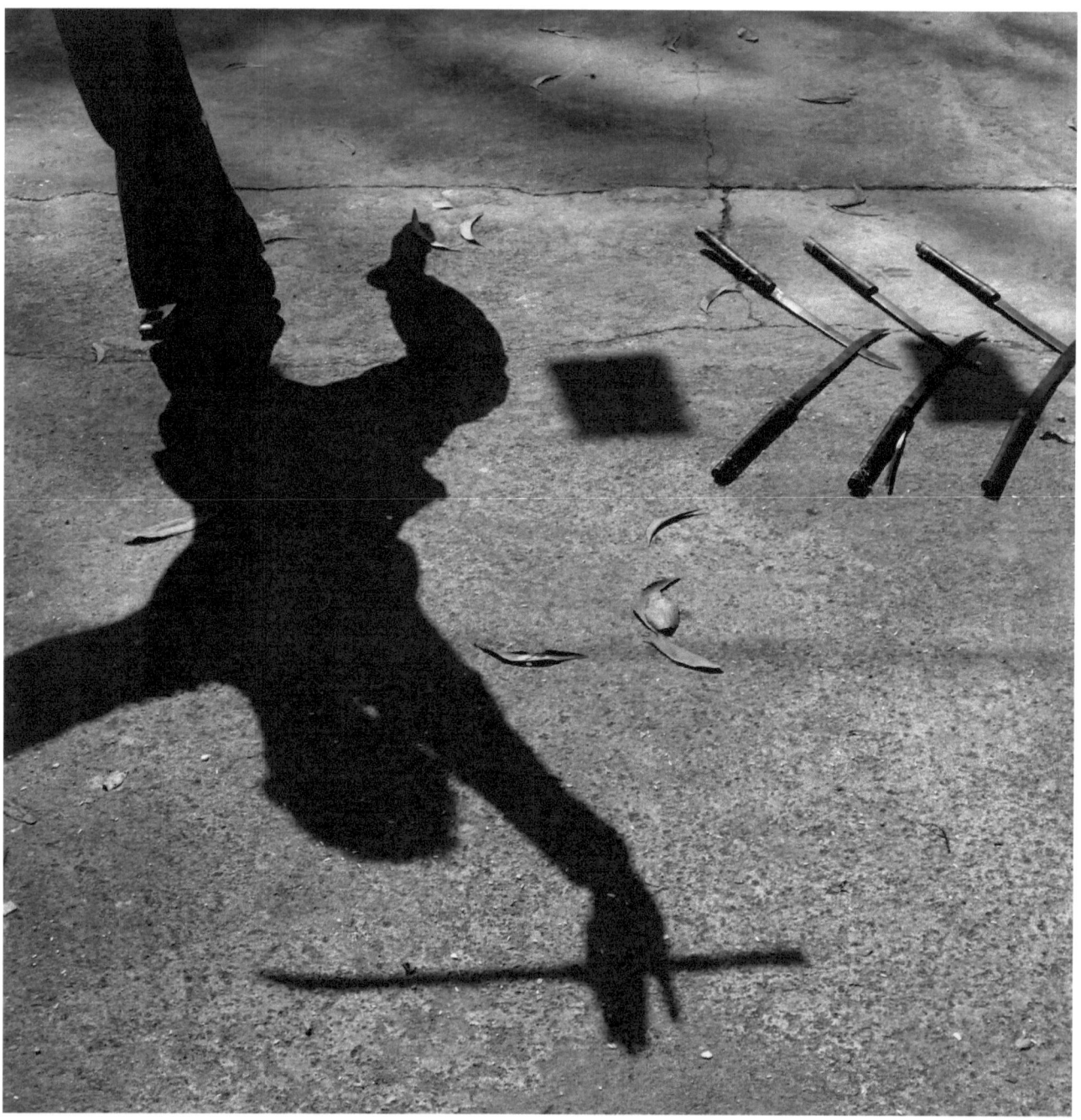

Fires on distant shores

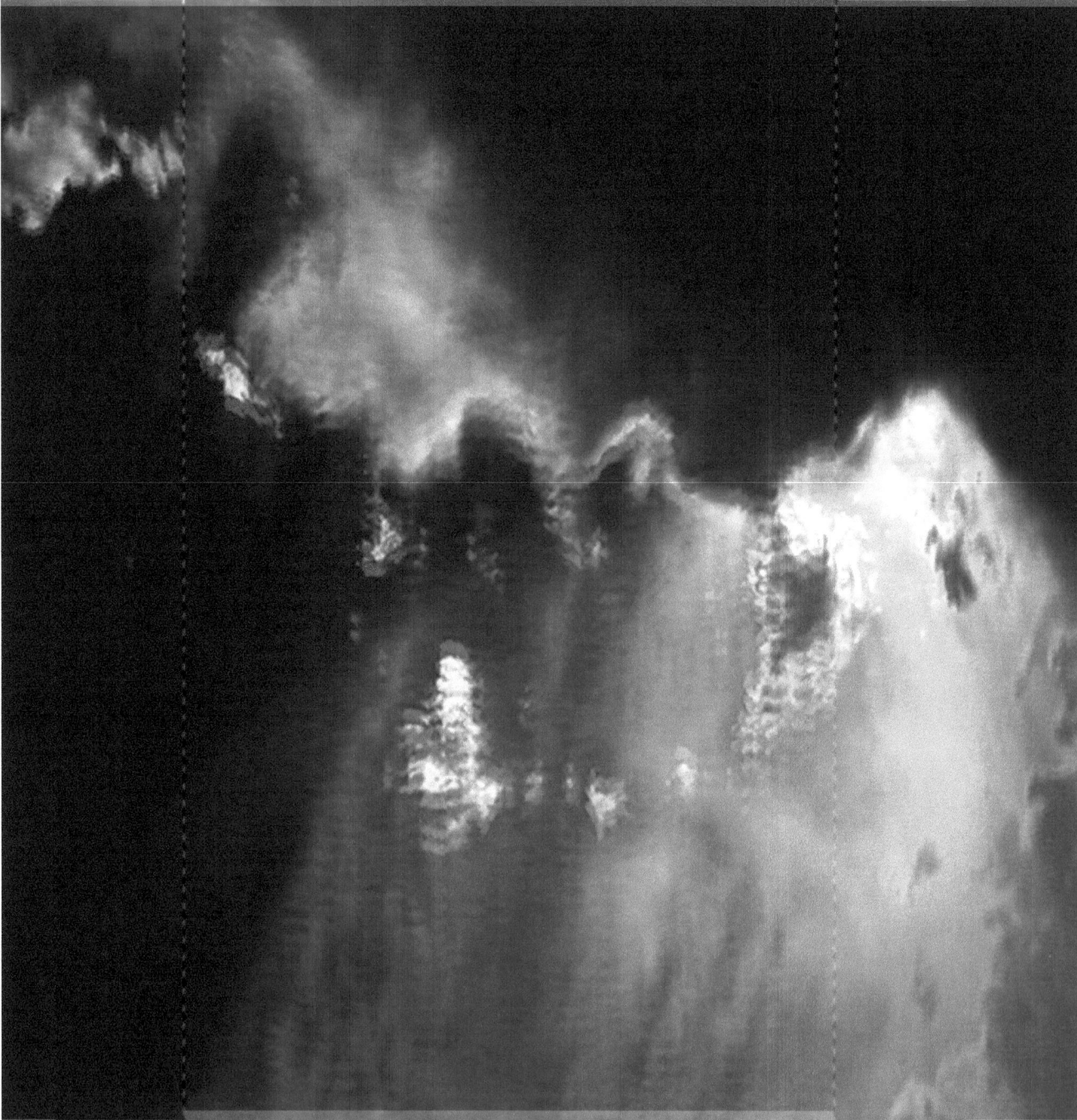

Tranquility in it all

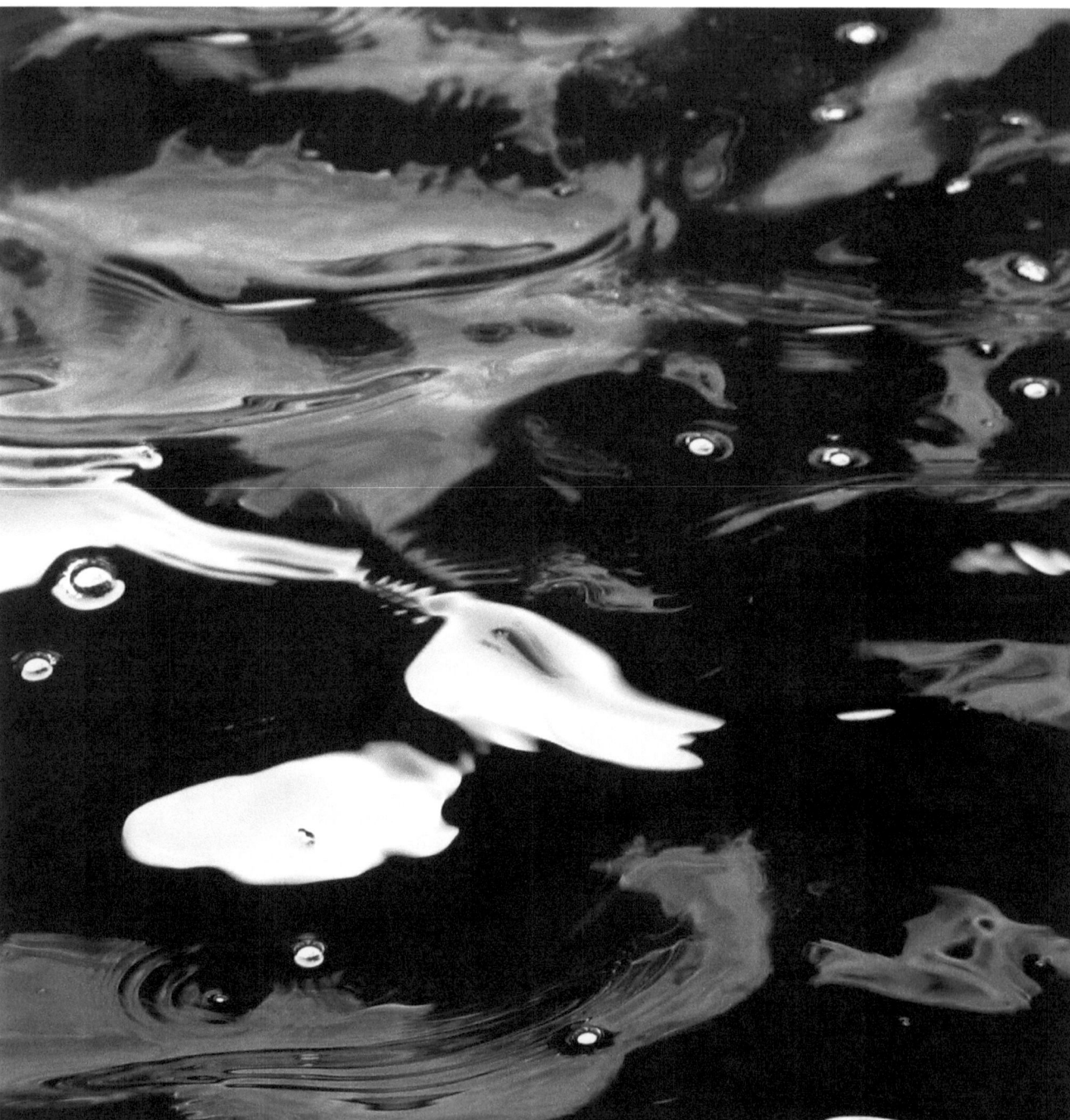

Imagine your grateful

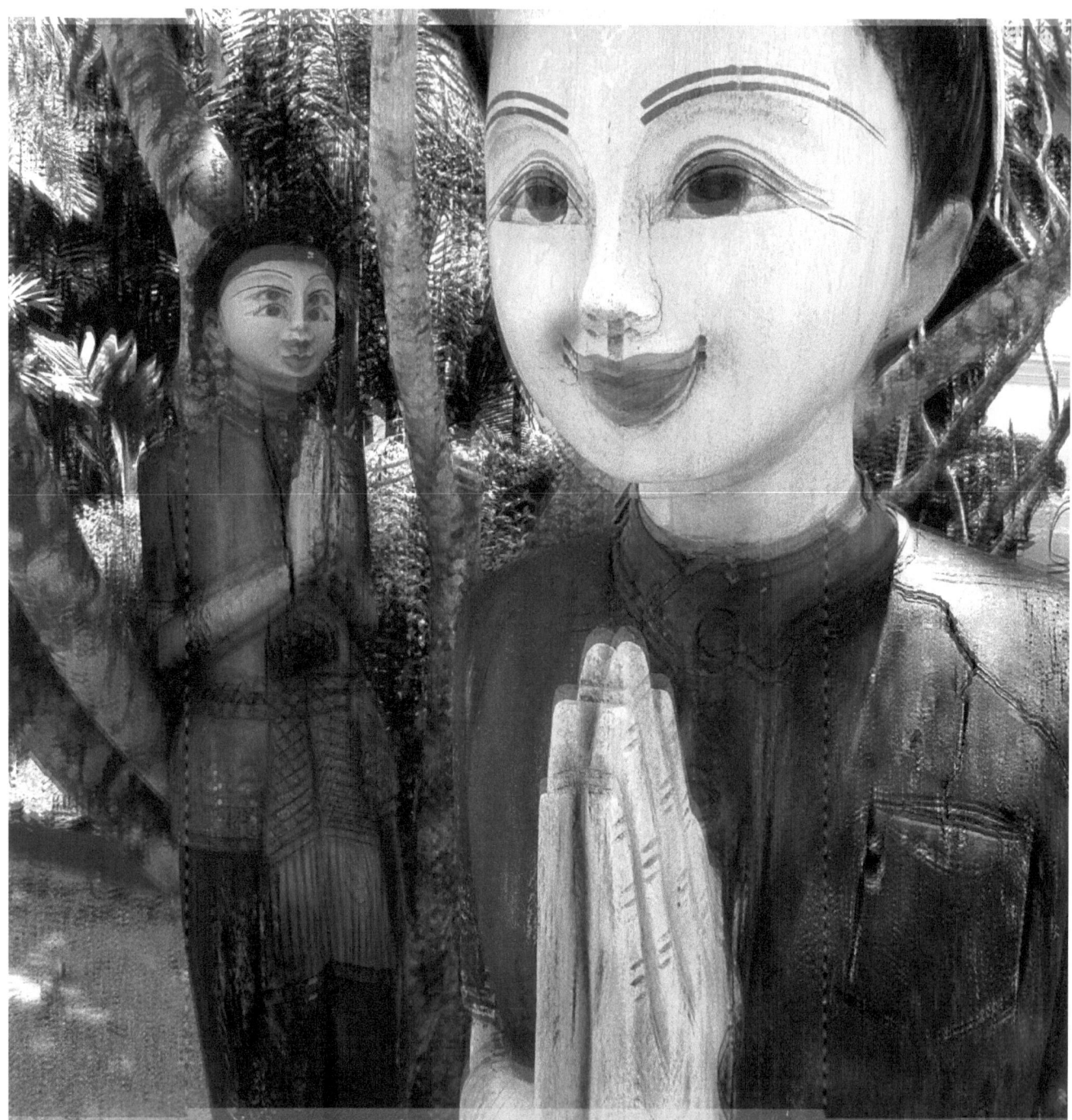

We are willing

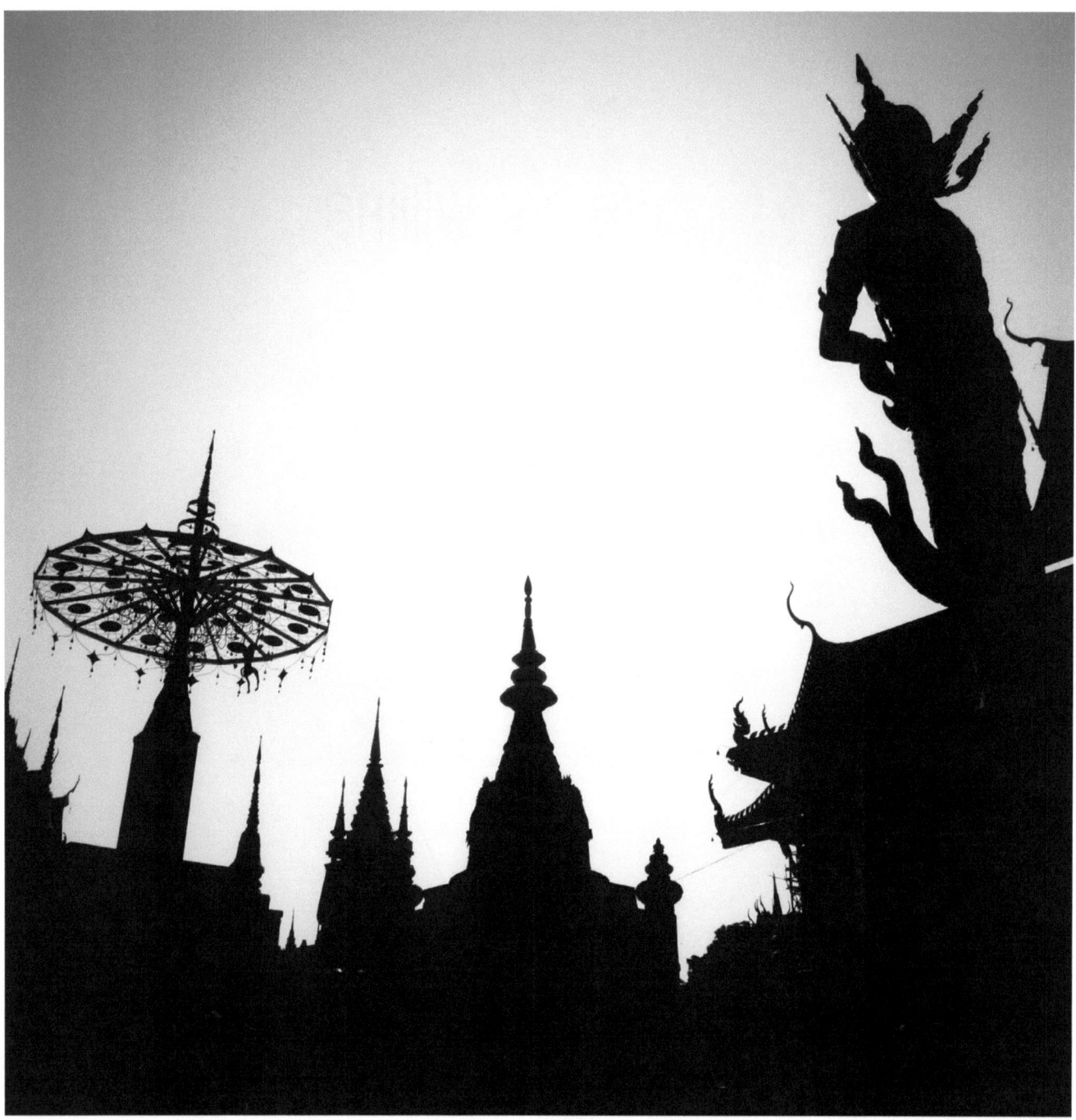

Words and pictures by Roditch

I believe in you

roditch@protonmail.com